A Book of Releases

David Kellin

Book Number_____

Date Started_____

ISBN: **1548381403**
ISBN-13: **978-1548381400**

INTRODUCTION

This a collection of a very simple model releases. They are collected here to allow you to carry them with you as you go. As a photographer, I have often wanted to have a person at an event sign a basic release. This book is an answer to my need.

NOTE:

I AM NOT A LAWYER. USE THESE WITH YOUR WISDOM AND KNOWLEDGE. THESE ARE NOT PRESENTED AS A LEGAL OPINION OR ADVICE.

In exchange for consideration received, I hereby give permission to_____to use my name and photographic likeness in all forms and media for advertising, trade, and any other lawful purposes.

Print Name:_____

Signature:_____

Date:_____

If Model is under 18:

I,_____am the parent/legal guardian of the individual named above, I have read this release and approve of its terms.

Print Name:_____

Signature:_____

Date:_____

Shoot/event_____

Description_____

In exchange for consideration received, I hereby give permission to_____to use my name and photographic likeness in all forms and media for advertising, trade, and any other lawful purposes.

Print Name:_____

Signature:_____

Date:_____

If Model is under 18:

I,_____am the parent/legal guardian of the individual named above, I have read this release and approve of its terms.

Print Name:_____

Signature:_____

Date:_____

Shoot/event_____

Description_____

In exchange for consideration received, I hereby give permission to_____to use my name and photographic likeness in all forms and media for advertising, trade, and any other lawful purposes.

Print Name:_____

Signature:_____

Date:_____

If Model is under 18:

I,_____am the parent/legal guardian of the individual named above, I have read this release and approve of its terms.

Print Name:_____

Signature:_____

Date:_____

Shoot/event_____

Description_____

In exchange for consideration received, I hereby give permission to_____to use my name and photographic likeness in all forms and media for advertising, trade, and any other lawful purposes.

Print Name:_____

Signature:_____

Date:_____

If Model is under 18:

I,_____am the parent/legal guardian of the individual named above, I have read this release and approve of its terms.

Print Name:_____

Signature:_____

Date:_____

Shoot/event_____

Description_____

Model Release

In exchange for consideration received, I hereby give permission to_____to use my name and photographic likeness in all forms and media for advertising, trade, and any other lawful purposes.

Print Name:_____

Signature:_____

Date:_____

If Model is under 18:

I,_____am the parent/legal guardian of the individual named above, I have read this release and approve of its terms.

Print Name:_____

Signature:_____

Date:_____

Shoot/event_____

Description_____

In exchange for consideration received, I hereby give permission to_____to use my name and photographic likeness in all forms and media for advertising, trade, and any other lawful purposes.

Print Name:_____

Signature:_____

Date:_____

If Model is under 18:

I,_____am the parent/legal guardian of the individual named above, I have read this release and approve of its terms.

Print Name:_____

Signature:_____

Date:_____

Shoot/event_____

Description_____

In exchange for consideration received, I hereby give permission to_____to use my name and photographic likeness in all forms and media for advertising, trade, and any other lawful purposes.

Print Name:_____

Signature:_____

Date:_____

If Model is under 18:

I,_____am the parent/legal guardian of the individual named above, I have read this release and approve of its terms.

Print Name:_____

Signature:_____

Date:_____

Shoot/event_____

Description_____

In exchange for consideration received, I hereby give permission to_____to use my name and photographic likeness in all forms and media for advertising, trade, and any other lawful purposes.

Print Name:_____

Signature:_____

Date:_____

If Model is under 18:

I,_____am the parent/legal guardian of the individual named above, I have read this release and approve of its terms.

Print Name:_____

Signature:_____

Date:_____

Shoot/event_____

Description_____

In exchange for consideration received, I hereby give permission to_____to use my name and photographic likeness in all forms and media for advertising, trade, and any other lawful purposes.

Print Name:_____

Signature:_____

Date:_____

If Model is under 18:

I,_____am the parent/legal guardian of the individual named above, I have read this release and approve of its terms.

Print Name:_____

Signature:_____

Date:_____

Shoot/event_____

Description_____

In exchange for consideration received, I hereby give permission to_____to use my name and photographic likeness in all forms and media for advertising, trade, and any other lawful purposes.

Print Name:_____

Signature:_____

Date:_____

If Model is under 18:

I,_____am the parent/legal guardian of the individual named above, I have read this release and approve of its terms.

Print Name:_____

Signature:_____

Date:_____

Shoot/event_____

Description_____

Model Release

In exchange for consideration received, I hereby give permission to_____to use my name and photographic likeness in all forms and media for advertising, trade, and any other lawful purposes.

Print Name:_____

Signature:_____

Date:_____

If Model is under 18:

I,_____am the parent/legal guardian of the individual named above, I have read this release and approve of its terms.

Print Name:_____

Signature:_____

Date:_____

Shoot/event_____

Description_____

In exchange for consideration received, I hereby give permission to_____to use my name and photographic likeness in all forms and media for advertising, trade, and any other lawful purposes.

Print Name:_____

Signature:_____

Date:_____

If Model is under 18:

I,_____am the parent/legal guardian of the individual named above, I have read this release and approve of its terms.

Print Name:_____

Signature:_____

Date:_____

Shoot/event_____

Description_____

In exchange for consideration received, I hereby give permission to_____to use my name and photographic likeness in all forms and media for advertising, trade, and any other lawful purposes.

Print Name:_____

Signature:_____

Date:_____

If Model is under 18:

I,_____am the parent/legal guardian of the individual named above, I have read this release and approve of its terms.

Print Name:_____

Signature:_____

Date:_____

Shoot/event_____

Description_____

In exchange for consideration received, I hereby give permission to_____to use my name and photographic likeness in all forms and media for advertising, trade, and any other lawful purposes.

Print Name:_____

Signature:_____

Date:_____

If Model is under 18:

I,_____am the parent/legal guardian of the individual named above, I have read this release and approve of its terms.

Print Name:_____

Signature:_____

Date:_____

Shoot/event_____

Description_____

In exchange for consideration received, I hereby give permission to_____to use my name and photographic likeness in all forms and media for advertising, trade, and any other lawful purposes.

Print Name:_____

Signature:_____

Date:_____

If Model is under 18:

I,_____am the parent/legal guardian of the individual named above, I have read this release and approve of its terms.

Print Name:_____

Signature:_____

Date:_____

Shoot/event_____

Description_____

In exchange for consideration received, I hereby give permission to_____to use my name and photographic likeness in all forms and media for advertising, trade, and any other lawful purposes.

Print Name:_____

Signature:_____

Date:_____

If Model is under 18:

I,_____am the parent/legal guardian of the individual named above, I have read this release and approve of its terms.

Print Name:_____

Signature:_____

Date:_____

Shoot/event_____

Description_____

Model Release

In exchange for consideration received, I hereby give permission to_____to use my name and photographic likeness in all forms and media for advertising, trade, and any other lawful purposes.

Print Name:_____

Signature:_____

Date:_____

If Model is under 18:

I,_____am the parent/legal guardian of the individual named above, I have read this release and approve of its terms.

Print Name:_____

Signature:_____

Date:_____

Shoot/event_____

Description_____

In exchange for consideration received, I hereby give permission to_____to use my name and photographic likeness in all forms and media for advertising, trade, and any other lawful purposes.

Print Name:_____

Signature:_____

Date:_____

If Model is under 18:

I,_____am the parent/legal guardian of the individual named above, I have read this release and approve of its terms.

Print Name:_____

Signature:_____

Date:_____

Shoot/event_____

Description_____

In exchange for consideration received, I hereby give permission to_____to use my name and photographic likeness in all forms and media for advertising, trade, and any other lawful purposes.

Print Name:_____

Signature:_____

Date:_____

If Model is under 18:

I,_____am the parent/legal guardian of the individual named above, I have read this release and approve of its terms.

Print Name:_____

Signature:_____

Date:_____

Shoot/event_____

Description_____

In exchange for consideration received, I hereby give permission to_____to use my name and photographic likeness in all forms and media for advertising, trade, and any other lawful purposes.

Print Name:_____

Signature:_____

Date:_____

If Model is under 18:

I,_____am the parent/legal guardian of the individual named above, I have read this release and approve of its terms.

Print Name:_____

Signature:_____

Date:_____

Shoot/event_____

Description_____

In exchange for consideration received, I hereby give permission to_____to use my name and photographic likeness in all forms and media for advertising, trade, and any other lawful purposes.

Print Name:_____

Signature:_____

Date:_____

If Model is under 18:

I,_____am the parent/legal guardian of the individual named above, I have read this release and approve of its terms.

Print Name:_____

Signature:_____

Date:_____

Shoot/event_____

Description_____

In exchange for consideration received, I hereby give permission to_____to use my name and photographic likeness in all forms and media for advertising, trade, and any other lawful purposes.

Print Name:_____

Signature:_____

Date:_____

If Model is under 18:

I,_____am the parent/legal guardian of the individual named above, I have read this release and approve of its terms.

Print Name:_____

Signature:_____

Date:_____

Shoot/event_____

Description_____

Model Release

In exchange for consideration received, I hereby give permission to_____to use my name and photographic likeness in all forms and media for advertising, trade, and any other lawful purposes.

Print Name:_____

Signature:_____

Date:_____

If Model is under 18:

I,_____am the parent/legal guardian of the individual named above, I have read this release and approve of its terms.

Print Name:_____

Signature:_____

Date:_____

Shoot/event_____

Description_____

In exchange for consideration received, I hereby give permission to_____to use my name and photographic likeness in all forms and media for advertising, trade, and any other lawful purposes.

Print Name:_____

Signature:_____

Date:_____

If Model is under 18:

I,_____am the parent/legal guardian of the individual named above, I have read this release and approve of its terms.

Print Name:_____

Signature:_____

Date:_____

Shoot/event_____

Description_____

In exchange for consideration received, I hereby give permission to_____to use my name and photographic likeness in all forms and media for advertising, trade, and any other lawful purposes.

Print Name:_____

Signature:_____

Date:_____

If Model is under 18:

I,_____am the parent/legal guardian of the individual named above, I have read this release and approve of its terms.

Print Name:_____

Signature:_____

Date:_____

Shoot/event_____

Description_____

In exchange for consideration received, I hereby give permission to_____to use my name and photographic likeness in all forms and media for advertising, trade, and any other lawful purposes.

Print Name:_____

Signature:_____

Date:_____

If Model is under 18:

I,_____am the parent/legal guardian of the individual named above, I have read this release and approve of its terms.

Print Name:_____

Signature:_____

Date:_____

Shoot/event_____

Description_____

In exchange for consideration received, I hereby give permission to_____to use my name and photographic likeness in all forms and media for advertising, trade, and any other lawful purposes.

Print Name:_____

Signature:_____

Date:_____

If Model is under 18:

I,_____am the parent/legal guardian of the individual named above, I have read this release and approve of its terms.

Print Name:_____

Signature:_____

Date:_____

Shoot/event_____

Description_____

In exchange for consideration received, I hereby give permission to_____to use my name and photographic likeness in all forms and media for advertising, trade, and any other lawful purposes.

Print Name:_____

Signature:_____

Date:_____

If Model is under 18:

I,_____am the parent/legal guardian of the individual named above, I have read this release and approve of its terms.

Print Name:_____

Signature:_____

Date:_____

Shoot/event_____

Description_____

Model Release

In exchange for consideration received, I hereby give permission to_____to use my name and photographic likeness in all forms and media for advertising, trade, and any other lawful purposes.

Print Name:_____

Signature:_____

Date:_____

If Model is under 18:

I,_____am the parent/legal guardian of the individual named above, I have read this release and approve of its terms.

Print Name:_____

Signature:_____

Date:_____

Shoot/event_____

Description_____

In exchange for consideration received, I hereby give permission to_____to use my name and photographic likeness in all forms and media for advertising, trade, and any other lawful purposes.

Print Name:_____

Signature:_____

Date:_____

If Model is under 18:

I,_____am the parent/legal guardian of the individual named above, I have read this release and approve of its terms.

Print Name:_____

Signature:_____

Date:_____

Shoot/event_____

Description_____

In exchange for consideration received, I hereby give permission to_____to use my name and photographic likeness in all forms and media for advertising, trade, and any other lawful purposes.

Print Name:_____

Signature:_____

Date:_____

If Model is under 18:

I,_____am the parent/legal guardian of the individual named above, I have read this release and approve of its terms.

Print Name:_____

Signature:_____

Date:_____

Shoot/event_____

Description_____

In exchange for consideration received, I hereby give permission to_____to use my name and photographic likeness in all forms and media for advertising, trade, and any other lawful purposes.

Print Name:_____

Signature:_____

Date:_____

If Model is under 18:

I,_____am the parent/legal guardian of the individual named above, I have read this release and approve of its terms.

Print Name:_____

Signature:_____

Date:_____

Shoot/event_____

Description_____

In exchange for consideration received, I hereby give permission to_____to use my name and photographic likeness in all forms and media for advertising, trade, and any other lawful purposes.

Print Name:_____

Signature:_____

Date:_____

If Model is under 18:

I,_____am the parent/legal guardian of the individual named above, I have read this release and approve of its terms.

Print Name:_____

Signature:_____

Date:_____

Shoot/event_____

Description_____

In exchange for consideration received, I hereby give permission to_____to use my name and photographic likeness in all forms and media for advertising, trade, and any other lawful purposes.

Print Name:_____

Signature:_____

Date:_____

If Model is under 18:

I,_____am the parent/legal guardian of the individual named above, I have read this release and approve of its terms.

Print Name:_____

Signature:_____

Date:_____

Shoot/event_____

Description_____

Model Release

In exchange for consideration received, I hereby give permission to_____to use my name and photographic likeness in all forms and media for advertising, trade, and any other lawful purposes.

Print Name:_____

Signature:_____

Date:_____

If Model is under 18:

I,_____am the parent/legal guardian of the individual named above, I have read this release and approve of its terms.

Print Name:_____

Signature:_____

Date:_____

Shoot/event_____

Description_____

In exchange for consideration received, I hereby give permission to_____to use my name and photographic likeness in all forms and media for advertising, trade, and any other lawful purposes.

Print Name:_____

Signature:_____

Date:_____

If Model is under 18:

I,_____am the parent/legal guardian of the individual named above, I have read this release and approve of its terms.

Print Name:_____

Signature:_____

Date:_____

Shoot/event_____

Description_____

In exchange for consideration received, I hereby give permission to_____to use my name and photographic likeness in all forms and media for advertising, trade, and any other lawful purposes.

Print Name:_____

Signature:_____

Date:_____

If Model is under 18:

I,_____am the parent/legal guardian of the individual named above, I have read this release and approve of its terms.

Print Name:_____

Signature:_____

Date:_____

--

Shoot/event_____

Description_____

In exchange for consideration received, I hereby give permission to_____to use my name and photographic likeness in all forms and media for advertising, trade, and any other lawful purposes.

Print Name:_____

Signature:_____

Date:_____

If Model is under 18:

I,_____am the parent/legal guardian of the individual named above, I have read this release and approve of its terms.

Print Name:_____

Signature:_____

Date:_____

--

Shoot/event_____

Description_____

In exchange for consideration received, I hereby give permission to_____to use my name and photographic likeness in all forms and media for advertising, trade, and any other lawful purposes.

Print Name:_____

Signature:_____

Date:_____

If Model is under 18:

I,_____am the parent/legal guardian of the individual named above, I have read this release and approve of its terms.

Print Name:_____

Signature:_____

Date:_____

Shoot/event_____

Description_____

In exchange for consideration received, I hereby give permission to_____to use my name and photographic likeness in all forms and media for advertising, trade, and any other lawful purposes.

Print Name:_____

Signature:_____

Date:_____

If Model is under 18:

I,_____am the parent/legal guardian of the individual named above, I have read this release and approve of its terms.

Print Name:_____

Signature:_____

Date:_____

Shoot/event_____

Description_____

In exchange for consideration received, I hereby give permission to_____to use my name and photographic likeness in all forms and media for advertising, trade, and any other lawful purposes.

Print Name:_____

Signature:_____

Date:_____

If Model is under 18:

I,_____am the parent/legal guardian of the individual named above, I have read this release and approve of its terms.

Print Name:_____

Signature:_____

Date:_____

Shoot/event_____

Description_____

In exchange for consideration received, I hereby give permission to_____to use my name and photographic likeness in all forms and media for advertising, trade, and any other lawful purposes.

Print Name:_____

Signature:_____

Date:_____

If Model is under 18:

I,_____am the parent/legal guardian of the individual named above, I have read this release and approve of its terms.

Print Name:_____

Signature:_____

Date:_____

Shoot/event_____

Description_____

Model Release

In exchange for consideration received, I hereby give permission to_____to use my name and photographic likeness in all forms and media for advertising, trade, and any other lawful purposes.

Print Name:_____

Signature:_____

Date:_____

If Model is under 18:

I,_____am the parent/legal guardian of the individual named above, I have read this release and approve of its terms.

Print Name:_____

Signature:_____

Date:_____

Shoot/event_____

Description_____

In exchange for consideration received, I hereby give permission to_____to use my name and photographic likeness in all forms and media for advertising, trade, and any other lawful purposes.

Print Name:_____

Signature:_____

Date:_____

If Model is under 18:

I,_____am the parent/legal guardian of the individual named above, I have read this release and approve of its terms.

Print Name:_____

Signature:_____

Date:_____

Shoot/event_____

Description_____

In exchange for consideration received, I hereby give permission to_____to use my name and photographic likeness in all forms and media for advertising, trade, and any other lawful purposes.

Print Name:_____

Signature:_____

Date:_____

If Model is under 18:

I,_____am the parent/legal guardian of the individual named above, I have read this release and approve of its terms.

Print Name:_____

Signature:_____

Date:_____

Shoot/event_____

Description_____

In exchange for consideration received, I hereby give permission to_____to use my name and photographic likeness in all forms and media for advertising, trade, and any other lawful purposes.

Print Name:_____

Signature:_____

Date:_____

If Model is under 18:

I,_____am the parent/legal guardian of the individual named above, I have read this release and approve of its terms.

Print Name:_____

Signature:_____

Date:_____

Shoot/event_____

Description_____

In exchange for consideration received, I hereby give permission to_____to use my name and photographic likeness in all forms and media for advertising, trade, and any other lawful purposes.

Print Name:_____

Signature:_____

Date:_____

If Model is under 18:

I,_____am the parent/legal guardian of the individual named above, I have read this release and approve of its terms.

Print Name:_____

Signature:_____

Date:_____

Shoot/event_____

Description_____

In exchange for consideration received, I hereby give permission to_____to use my name and photographic likeness in all forms and media for advertising, trade, and any other lawful purposes.

Print Name:_____

Signature:_____

Date:_____

If Model is under 18:

I,_____am the parent/legal guardian of the individual named above, I have read this release and approve of its terms.

Print Name:_____

Signature:_____

Date:_____

Shoot/event_____

Description_____

Model Release

In exchange for consideration received, I hereby give permission to_____to use my name and photographic likeness in all forms and media for advertising, trade, and any other lawful purposes.

Print Name:_____

Signature:_____

Date:_____

If Model is under 18:

I,_____am the parent/legal guardian of the individual named above, I have read this release and approve of its terms.

Print Name:_____

Signature:_____

Date:_____

Shoot/event_____

Description_____

In exchange for consideration received, I hereby give permission to_____to use my name and photographic likeness in all forms and media for advertising, trade, and any other lawful purposes.

Print Name:_____

Signature:_____

Date:_____

If Model is under 18:

I,_____am the parent/legal guardian of the individual named above, I have read this release and approve of its terms.

Print Name:_____

Signature:_____

Date:_____

Shoot/event_____

Description_____

In exchange for consideration received, I hereby give permission to_____to use my name and photographic likeness in all forms and media for advertising, trade, and any other lawful purposes.

Print Name:_____

Signature:_____

Date:_____

If Model is under 18:

I,_____am the parent/legal guardian of the individual named above, I have read this release and approve of its terms.

Print Name:_____

Signature:_____

Date:_____

Shoot/event_____

Description_____

In exchange for consideration received, I hereby give permission to_____to use my name and photographic likeness in all forms and media for advertising, trade, and any other lawful purposes.

Print Name:_____

Signature:_____

Date:_____

If Model is under 18:

I,_____am the parent/legal guardian of the individual named above, I have read this release and approve of its terms.

Print Name:_____

Signature:_____

Date:_____

Shoot/event_____

Description_____

In exchange for consideration received, I hereby give permission to_____to use my name and photographic likeness in all forms and media for advertising, trade, and any other lawful purposes.

Print Name:_____

Signature:_____

Date:_____

If Model is under 18:

I,_____am the parent/legal guardian of the individual named above, I have read this release and approve of its terms.

Print Name:_____

Signature:_____

Date:_____

Shoot/event_____

Description_____

In exchange for consideration received, I hereby give permission to_____to use my name and photographic likeness in all forms and media for advertising, trade, and any other lawful purposes.

Print Name:_____

Signature:_____

Date:_____

If Model is under 18:

I,_____am the parent/legal guardian of the individual named above, I have read this release and approve of its terms.

Print Name:_____

Signature:_____

Date:_____

Shoot/event_____

Description_____

Model Release

In exchange for consideration received, I hereby give permission to_____to use my name and photographic likeness in all forms and media for advertising, trade, and any other lawful purposes.

Print Name:_____

Signature:_____

Date:_____

If Model is under 18:

I,_____am the parent/legal guardian of the individual named above, I have read this release and approve of its terms.

Print Name:_____

Signature:_____

Date:_____

Shoot/event_____

Description_____

In exchange for consideration received, I hereby give permission to_____to use my name and photographic likeness in all forms and media for advertising, trade, and any other lawful purposes.

Print Name:_____

Signature:_____

Date:_____

If Model is under 18:

I,_____am the parent/legal guardian of the individual named above, I have read this release and approve of its terms.

Print Name:_____

Signature:_____

Date:_____

Shoot/event_____

Description_____

In exchange for consideration received, I hereby give permission to_____to use my name and photographic likeness in all forms and media for advertising, trade, and any other lawful purposes.

Print Name:_____

Signature:_____

Date:_____

If Model is under 18:

I,_____am the parent/legal guardian of the individual named above, I have read this release and approve of its terms.

Print Name:_____

Signature:_____

Date:_____

Shoot/event_____

Description_____

In exchange for consideration received, I hereby give permission to_____to use my name and photographic likeness in all forms and media for advertising, trade, and any other lawful purposes.

Print Name:_____

Signature:_____

Date:_____

If Model is under 18:

I,_____am the parent/legal guardian of the individual named above, I have read this release and approve of its terms.

Print Name:_____

Signature:_____

Date:_____

Shoot/event_____

Description_____

In exchange for consideration received, I hereby give permission to_____to use my name and photographic likeness in all forms and media for advertising, trade, and any other lawful purposes.

Print Name:_____

Signature:_____

Date:_____

If Model is under 18:

I,_____am the parent/legal guardian of the individual named above, I have read this release and approve of its terms.

Print Name:_____

Signature:_____

Date:_____

Shoot/event_____

Description_____

In exchange for consideration received, I hereby give permission to_____to use my name and photographic likeness in all forms and media for advertising, trade, and any other lawful purposes.

Print Name:_____

Signature:_____

Date:_____

If Model is under 18:

I,_____am the parent/legal guardian of the individual named above, I have read this release and approve of its terms.

Print Name:_____

Signature:_____

Date:_____

Shoot/event_____

Description_____

Model Release

In exchange for consideration received, I hereby give permission to_____to use my name and photographic likeness in all forms and media for advertising, trade, and any other lawful purposes.

Print Name:_____

Signature:_____

Date:_____

If Model is under 18:

I,_____am the parent/legal guardian of the individual named above, I have read this release and approve of its terms.

Print Name:_____

Signature:_____

Date:_____

Shoot/event_____

Description_____

In exchange for consideration received, I hereby give permission to_____to use my name and photographic likeness in all forms and media for advertising, trade, and any other lawful purposes.

Print Name:_____

Signature:_____

Date:_____

If Model is under 18:

I,_____am the parent/legal guardian of the individual named above, I have read this release and approve of its terms.

Print Name:_____

Signature:_____

Date:_____

Shoot/event_____

Description_____

In exchange for consideration received, I hereby give permission to_____to use my name and photographic likeness in all forms and media for advertising, trade, and any other lawful purposes.

Print Name:_____

Signature:_____

Date:_____

If Model is under 18:

I,_____am the parent/legal guardian of the individual named above, I have read this release and approve of its terms.

Print Name:_____

Signature:_____

Date:_____

Shoot/event_____

Description_____

In exchange for consideration received, I hereby give permission to_____to use my name and photographic likeness in all forms and media for advertising, trade, and any other lawful purposes.

Print Name:_____

Signature:_____

Date:_____

If Model is under 18:

I,_____am the parent/legal guardian of the individual named above, I have read this release and approve of its terms.

Print Name:_____

Signature:_____

Date:_____

Shoot/event_____

Description_____

In exchange for consideration received, I hereby give permission to_____to use my name and photographic likeness in all forms and media for advertising, trade, and any other lawful purposes.

Print Name:_____

Signature:_____

Date:_____

If Model is under 18:

I,_____am the parent/legal guardian of the individual named above, I have read this release and approve of its terms.

Print Name:_____

Signature:_____

Date:_____

Shoot/event_____

Description_____

In exchange for consideration received, I hereby give permission to_____to use my name and photographic likeness in all forms and media for advertising, trade, and any other lawful purposes.

Print Name:_____

Signature:_____

Date:_____

If Model is under 18:

I,_____am the parent/legal guardian of the individual named above, I have read this release and approve of its terms.

Print Name:_____

Signature:_____

Date:_____

Shoot/event_____

Description_____

Model Release

In exchange for consideration received, I hereby give permission to_____to use my name and photographic likeness in all forms and media for advertising, trade, and any other lawful purposes.

Print Name:_____

Signature:_____

Date:_____

If Model is under 18:

I,_____am the parent/legal guardian of the individual named above, I have read this release and approve of its terms.

Print Name:_____

Signature:_____

Date:_____

Shoot/event_____

Description_____

In exchange for consideration received, I hereby give permission to_____to use my name and photographic likeness in all forms and media for advertising, trade, and any other lawful purposes.

Print Name:_____

Signature:_____

Date:_____

If Model is under 18:

I,_____am the parent/legal guardian of the individual named above, I have read this release and approve of its terms.

Print Name:_____

Signature:_____

Date:_____

Shoot/event_____

Description_____

In exchange for consideration received, I hereby give permission to_____to use my name and photographic likeness in all forms and media for advertising, trade, and any other lawful purposes.

Print Name:_____

Signature:_____

Date:_____

If Model is under 18:

I,_____am the parent/legal guardian of the individual named above, I have read this release and approve of its terms.

Print Name:_____

Signature:_____

Date:_____

Shoot/event_____

Description_____

In exchange for consideration received, I hereby give permission to_____to use my name and photographic likeness in all forms and media for advertising, trade, and any other lawful purposes.

Print Name:_____

Signature:_____

Date:_____

If Model is under 18:

I,_____am the parent/legal guardian of the individual named above, I have read this release and approve of its terms.

Print Name:_____

Signature:_____

Date:_____

Shoot/event_____

Description_____

In exchange for consideration received, I hereby give permission to_____to use my name and photographic likeness in all forms and media for advertising, trade, and any other lawful purposes.

Print Name:_____

Signature:_____

Date:_____

If Model is under 18:

I,_____am the parent/legal guardian of the individual named above, I have read this release and approve of its terms.

Print Name:_____

Signature:_____

Date:_____

Shoot/event_____

Description_____

In exchange for consideration received, I hereby give permission to_____to use my name and photographic likeness in all forms and media for advertising, trade, and any other lawful purposes.

Print Name:_____

Signature:_____

Date:_____

If Model is under 18:

I,_____am the parent/legal guardian of the individual named above, I have read this release and approve of its terms.

Print Name:_____

Signature:_____

Date:_____

Shoot/event_____

Description_____

Model Release

In exchange for consideration received, I hereby give permission to_____to use my name and photographic likeness in all forms and media for advertising, trade, and any other lawful purposes.

Print Name:_____

Signature:_____

Date:_____

If Model is under 18:

I,_____am the parent/legal guardian of the individual named above, I have read this release and approve of its terms.

Print Name:_____

Signature:_____

Date:_____

Shoot/event_____

Description_____

In exchange for consideration received, I hereby give permission to_____to use my name and photographic likeness in all forms and media for advertising, trade, and any other lawful purposes.

Print Name:_____

Signature:_____

Date:_____

If Model is under 18:

I,_____am the parent/legal guardian of the individual named above, I have read this release and approve of its terms.

Print Name:_____

Signature:_____

Date:_____

Shoot/event_____

Description_____

In exchange for consideration received, I hereby give permission to_____to use my name and photographic likeness in all forms and media for advertising, trade, and any other lawful purposes.

Print Name:_____

Signature:_____

Date:_____

If Model is under 18:

I,_____am the parent/legal guardian of the individual named above, I have read this release and approve of its terms.

Print Name:_____

Signature:_____

Date:_____

Shoot/event_____

Description_____

In exchange for consideration received, I hereby give permission to_____to use my name and photographic likeness in all forms and media for advertising, trade, and any other lawful purposes.

Print Name:_____

Signature:_____

Date:_____

If Model is under 18:

I,_____am the parent/legal guardian of the individual named above, I have read this release and approve of its terms.

Print Name:_____

Signature:_____

Date:_____

Shoot/event_____

Description_____

In exchange for consideration received, I hereby give permission to_____to use my name and photographic likeness in all forms and media for advertising, trade, and any other lawful purposes.

Print Name:_____

Signature:_____

Date:_____

If Model is under 18:

I,_____am the parent/legal guardian of the individual named above, I have read this release and approve of its terms.

Print Name:_____

Signature:_____

Date:_____

Shoot/event_____

Description_____

In exchange for consideration received, I hereby give permission to_____to use my name and photographic likeness in all forms and media for advertising, trade, and any other lawful purposes.

Print Name:_____

Signature:_____

Date:_____

If Model is under 18:

I,_____am the parent/legal guardian of the individual named above, I have read this release and approve of its terms.

Print Name:_____

Signature:_____

Date:_____

Shoot/event_____

Description_____

Model Release

In exchange for consideration received, I hereby give permission to_____to use my name and photographic likeness in all forms and media for advertising, trade, and any other lawful purposes.

Print Name:_____

Signature:_____

Date:_____

If Model is under 18:

I,_____am the parent/legal guardian of the individual named above, I have read this release and approve of its terms.

Print Name:_____

Signature:_____

Date:_____

Shoot/event_____

Description_____

In exchange for consideration received, I hereby give permission to_____to use my name and photographic likeness in all forms and media for advertising, trade, and any other lawful purposes.

Print Name:_____

Signature:_____

Date:_____

If Model is under 18:

I,_____am the parent/legal guardian of the individual named above, I have read this release and approve of its terms.

Print Name:_____

Signature:_____

Date:_____

Shoot/event_____

Description_____

In exchange for consideration received, I hereby give permission to_____to use my name and photographic likeness in all forms and media for advertising, trade, and any other lawful purposes.

Print Name:_____

Signature:_____

Date:_____

If Model is under 18:

I,_____am the parent/legal guardian of the individual named above, I have read this release and approve of its terms.

Print Name:_____

Signature:_____

Date:_____

Shoot/event_____

Description_____

In exchange for consideration received, I hereby give permission to_____to use my name and photographic likeness in all forms and media for advertising, trade, and any other lawful purposes.

Print Name:_____

Signature:_____

Date:_____

If Model is under 18:

I,_____am the parent/legal guardian of the individual named above, I have read this release and approve of its terms.

Print Name:_____

Signature:_____

Date:_____

Shoot/event_____

Description_____

In exchange for consideration received, I hereby give permission to_____to use my name and photographic likeness in all forms and media for advertising, trade, and any other lawful purposes.

Print Name:_____

Signature:_____

Date:_____

If Model is under 18:

I,_____am the parent/legal guardian of the individual named above, I have read this release and approve of its terms.

Print Name:_____

Signature:_____

Date:_____

Shoot/event_____

Description_____

In exchange for consideration received, I hereby give permission to_____to use my name and photographic likeness in all forms and media for advertising, trade, and any other lawful purposes.

Print Name:_____

Signature:_____

Date:_____

If Model is under 18:

I,_____am the parent/legal guardian of the individual named above, I have read this release and approve of its terms.

Print Name:_____

Signature:_____

Date:_____

Shoot/event_____

Description_____

Model Release

In exchange for consideration received, I hereby give permission to_____to use my name and photographic likeness in all forms and media for advertising, trade, and any other lawful purposes.

Print Name:_____

Signature:_____

Date:_____

If Model is under 18:

I,_____am the parent/legal guardian of the individual named above, I have read this release and approve of its terms.

Print Name:_____

Signature:_____

Date:_____

Shoot/event_____

Description_____

In exchange for consideration received, I hereby give permission to_____to use my name and photographic likeness in all forms and media for advertising, trade, and any other lawful purposes.

Print Name:_____

Signature:_____

Date:_____

If Model is under 18:

I,_____am the parent/legal guardian of the individual named above, I have read this release and approve of its terms.

Print Name:_____

Signature:_____

Date:_____

Shoot/event_____

Description_____

In exchange for consideration received, I hereby give permission to_____to use my name and photographic likeness in all forms and media for advertising, trade, and any other lawful purposes.

Print Name:_____

Signature:_____

Date:_____

If Model is under 18:

I,_____am the parent/legal guardian of the individual named above, I have read this release and approve of its terms.

Print Name:_____

Signature:_____

Date:_____

Shoot/event_____

Description_____

In exchange for consideration received, I hereby give permission to_____to use my name and photographic likeness in all forms and media for advertising, trade, and any other lawful purposes.

Print Name:_____

Signature:_____

Date:_____

If Model is under 18:

I,_____am the parent/legal guardian of the individual named above, I have read this release and approve of its terms.

Print Name:_____

Signature:_____

Date:_____

Shoot/event_____

Description_____

In exchange for consideration received, I hereby give permission to_____to use my name and photographic likeness in all forms and media for advertising, trade, and any other lawful purposes.

Print Name:_____

Signature:_____

Date:_____

If Model is under 18:

I,_____am the parent/legal guardian of the individual named above, I have read this release and approve of its terms.

Print Name:_____

Signature:_____

Date:_____

Shoot/event_____

Description_____

In exchange for consideration received, I hereby give permission to_____to use my name and photographic likeness in all forms and media for advertising, trade, and any other lawful purposes.

Print Name:_____

Signature:_____

Date:_____

If Model is under 18:

I,_____am the parent/legal guardian of the individual named above, I have read this release and approve of its terms.

Print Name:_____

Signature:_____

Date:_____

Shoot/event_____

Description_____

Model Release

In exchange for consideration received, I hereby give permission to_____to use my name and photographic likeness in all forms and media for advertising, trade, and any other lawful purposes.

Print Name:_____

Signature:_____

Date:_____

If Model is under 18:

I,_____am the parent/legal guardian of the individual named above, I have read this release and approve of its terms.

Print Name:_____

Signature:_____

Date:_____

Shoot/event_____

Description_____

In exchange for consideration received, I hereby give permission to_____to use my name and photographic likeness in all forms and media for advertising, trade, and any other lawful purposes.

Print Name:_____

Signature:_____

Date:_____

If Model is under 18:

I,_____am the parent/legal guardian of the individual named above, I have read this release and approve of its terms.

Print Name:_____

Signature:_____

Date:_____

Shoot/event_____

Description_____

In exchange for consideration received, I hereby give permission to_____to use my name and photographic likeness in all forms and media for advertising, trade, and any other lawful purposes.

Print Name:_____

Signature:_____

Date:_____

If Model is under 18:

I,_____am the parent/legal guardian of the individual named above, I have read this release and approve of its terms.

Print Name:_____

Signature:_____

Date:_____

Shoot/event_____

Description_____

In exchange for consideration received, I hereby give permission to_____to use my name and photographic likeness in all forms and media for advertising, trade, and any other lawful purposes.

Print Name:_____

Signature:_____

Date:_____

If Model is under 18:

I,_____am the parent/legal guardian of the individual named above, I have read this release and approve of its terms.

Print Name:_____

Signature:_____

Date:_____

Shoot/event_____

Description_____

In exchange for consideration received, I hereby give permission to_____to use my name and photographic likeness in all forms and media for advertising, trade, and any other lawful purposes.

Print Name:_____

Signature:_____

Date:_____

If Model is under 18:

I,_____am the parent/legal guardian of the individual named above, I have read this release and approve of its terms.

Print Name:_____

Signature:_____

Date:_____

Shoot/event_____

Description_____

About David Kellin

David is a freelance Photographer and Photojournalist in South Carolina. He submits to local newspapers and news stations. Largely an event photographer, he works to capture moments as they happen rather than posed shots.

David Kellin
PO Box 851
Kershaw, SC 29067
kellinphotog@gmail.com